Made in United States
North Haven, CT
17 December 2024

62701988R00079